For Hannah & Emily x
– SGC

Sital Gorasia Chapman is passionate about bringing maths to life for kids. She worked in finance before becoming a children's author.

Consultant Steph King works with primary educators to improve maths teaching and learning in the classroom. She has written many maths books for children.

Author Sital Gorasia Chapman
Primary Mathematics Adviser Steph King
Illustrator Susanna Rumiz
Editors Laura Gilbert, Rea Pikula
Senior Designer Rachael Parfitt Hunt
Project Art Editor Victoria Palastanga
Production Editor Becky Fallowfield
Production Controller Magda Bojko
Jacket Coordinator Elin Woosnam
Managing Editor Penny Smith
Managing Art Editor Anna Hall
Art Director Mabel Chan
Publisher Francesca Young

First published in Great Britain in 2025 by
Dorling Kindersley Limited
20 Vauxhall Bridge Road
London SW1V 2SA

The authorised representative in the EEA is
Dorling Kindersley Verlag GmbH. Arnulfstr. 124,
80636 Munich, Germany

10 9 8 7 6 5 4 3 2 1
001–342125–Sep/2025

A CIP catalogue record for this book is available from the British Library.
ISBN: 978-0-2416-8631-7

Printed and bound in China

www.dk.com

This book was made with Forest Stewardship Council™ certified paper – one small step in DK's commitment to a sustainable future.
Learn more at www.dk.com/uk/information/sustainability

The Maths Adventurers

Go Looking for Bugs

Beep and Boots were in the woods
for the Annual Big Bug Spot.
They'd mark them on their spotter cards.
They hoped to see a lot.

Beep's dream had always been to see
a creature rarer than rare –
a blushing pink grasshopper.
She wished they'd find one there.

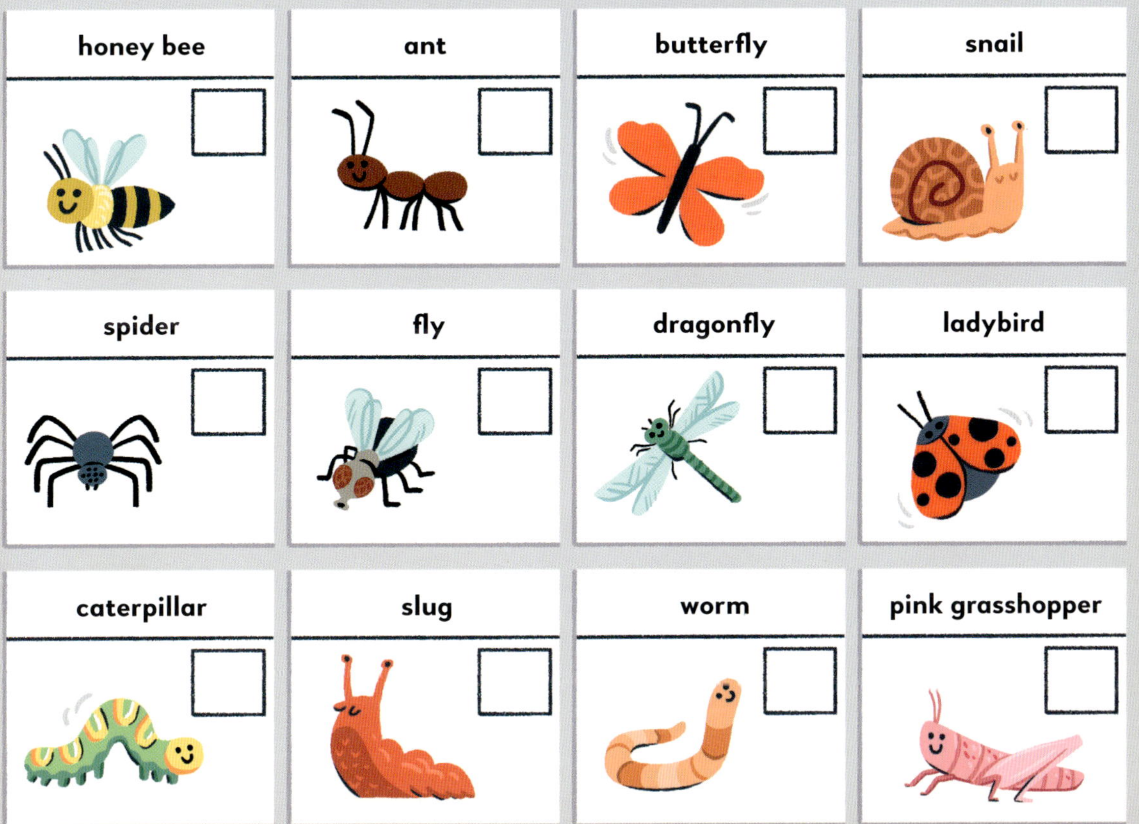

An array arranges objects in equal rows and columns. You can use it to help you solve multiplication problems. The spotter card has 3 rows of 4 bugs. That's 12 bugs in total.

They looked up in the branches
and low down on the ground.
But where were all the insects?

And what was that buzzing sound?

They tracked the noise down quickly
to a patch of flowers blooming,
where sweet-smelling nectar
kept lots of busy bees zooming.

There were two bees in every flower
and 10 flowers by the trees.
Boots worked out the total.
There were 20 honey bees.

You can think of multiplication as repeated addition.
We can say that 5 groups of 2 honey bees equals 10 honey bees.

Can you think how you can use repeated addition to show
10 groups of 2 honey bees?

Beep wrote down the number,
then noticed something weird.
A line of leaves marched up a hill
and swiftly disappeared!

"What's going on?" Beep wondered,
as she took a peek beneath.
And there she found three strong ants
carrying each leaf.

Ten times they watched it happen.
There were 30 ants in all.
Then excitedly Boots pointed
at something pink above the wall.

The symbol for multiplication is X.
You can multiply numbers in any order 5 x 3 and 3 x 5 both equal 15.

Can you use the symbol X to show the number of ants that Beep has found?

A flight of lovely butterflies,
five in every hue –
orange, pink, and purple,
red, white, green, and blue.

They filled the sky with colour
and then away they flew.
Beep marked them on her spotter card,
then looked for another clue.

She took her magnifying glass
and followed a slimy trail.
Left, then right, then left again.
It led her to a snail.

The snail chomped on a mushroom.
His friends were there to share.
Seven mushrooms on the grass.
On each a snail pair.

Beep found a silky spider's web,
four flies caught by the beast.
Boots then spotted a second one
with another four-fly feast!

They'd found six different types of bugs,
another six to find.
But of the rare pink grasshopper,
still there was no sign.

Big Bug Spotter Card

honey bee	ant	butterfly	snail
20	30	35	14
	fly	dragonfly	ladybird
2	8		
caterpillar	slug	worm	pink grass

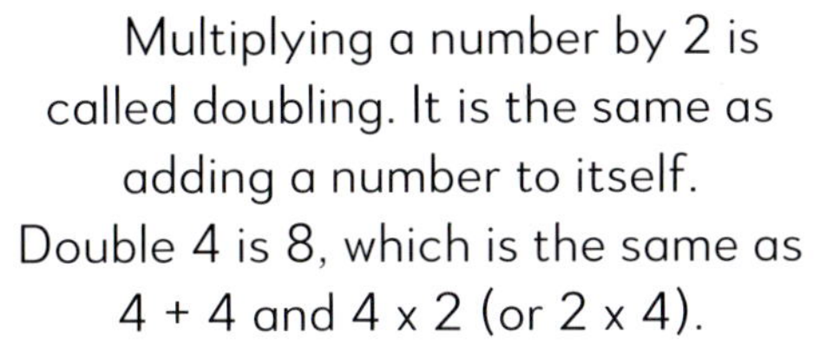

Multiplying a number by 2 is called doubling. It is the same as adding a number to itself. Double 4 is 8, which is the same as 4 + 4 and 4 x 2 (or 2 x 4).

Beep was disappointed.
Boots was extra kind.
They rested on a toppled trunk...

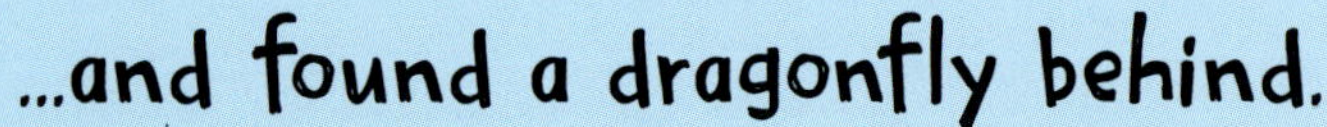
...and found a dragonfly behind.

It spread two pairs of wings out wide
and flew into the sky,
where three seven-spotted ladybirds
were flitting way up high.

Beep discovered six caterpillars
crawling in some rubble.
Boots noticed another six hiding,
making the total double.

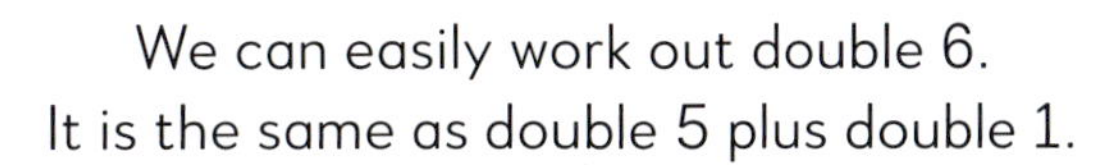

We can easily work out double 6.
It is the same as double 5 plus double 1.

Double 5 is 10 and double 1 is 2, so double 6 is 12.

They found a slug eating a shrub,
five wiggly worms under a stone.
Beep lifted up another two rocks
and found they weren't alone.

Beep and Boots had searched all day.
Their hunt was nearly done.
They'd found almost all the bugs.
But not the most special one.

Then suddenly Boots ears pricked up
as she heard a tell-tale sound –
a pink grasshopper's chirping song.
Once more they searched around.

They looked at leaves and under logs.
Explored the damp
and dark.

They dug up dirt, examined rocks,
checked in bushes
and on bark.

They were tired and frustrated.
"We've looked everywhere!" Beep said.
And then her little eyes lit up
as a plan popped in her head!

They lay some tasty nibbles
near the grass just by their feet...

...and a cloud of hungry grasshoppers descended on the treat!

And there, right in the middle
of the massive group of green,
the bug that Beep had dreamed of –
a pink grasshopper queen.

GLOSSARY

Column – objects arranged in a vertical line

Row – objects arranged in a horizontal line

Array – a group of objects arranged in equal rows and columns

Group – a number of objects

Equal – the same amount

Multiplication – when a number is multiplied by another so making copies. This can be seen as repeated addition

4 x 3 = 3 + 3 + 3 + 3

1 x 3 = 3
2 x 3 = 6
3 x 3 = 9
4 x 3 = 12
5 x 3 = 15

Times table – a list of multiples of a number

Repeated addition – adding a number repeatedly to itself

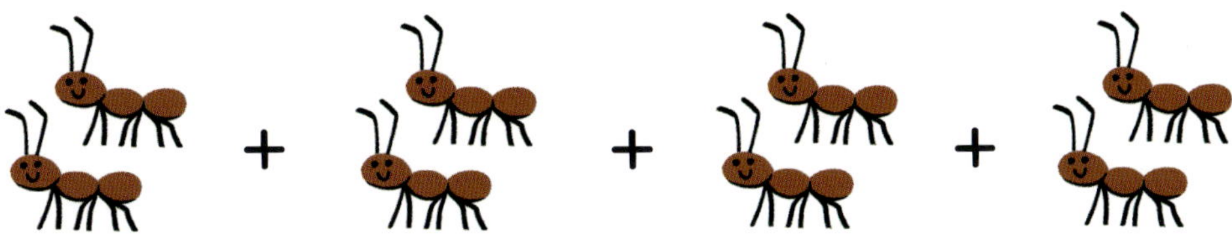

Double – multiply by two. For example, 2 doubled is the same as 2 x 2

QUESTIONS

1. What is 8 times 2?

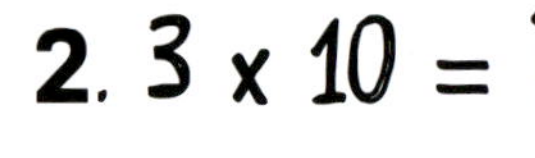

2. 3 x 10 = ?

3. What is 6 x 3? What is 3 x 6?

4. A dragonfly has two pairs of wings. How many wings do 10 dragonflies have?

5. What is 9 doubled?

6. Which of these is not the same?

a. 4 x 2

b. 2 x 4

c. 2 + 2 + 2 + 2

d. 4 + 4 + 4

7. An ant has 6 legs. How many legs do 5 ants have?

8. A grasshopper takes 5 minutes to eat 1 raspberry. How many raspberries can it eat in 1 hour?

9. A bee visits 10 different flowers to collect nectar. It spends 2 minutes on each flower before returning to its hive. How long does it spend collecting nectar?

10. 5 caterpillars eat 3 cabbage leaves each. How many cabbage leaves are eaten all together?

ANSWERS

1. 16
2. 30
3. Both answers are 18
4. 40
5. 18
6. d
7. 30
8. 12 raspberries
9. 20 minutes
10. 15 cabbage leaves

⚠ If you spot a bug, don't touch! They like to be left alone.